CHESTER

Edited by Michelle Warrington

First published in Great Britain in 1999 by
POETRY NOW YOUNG WRITERS
Remus House, Coltsfoot Drive,
Woodston,
Peterborough, PE2 9JX
Telephone (01733) 890066

HB ISBN 0 75430 393 4
SB ISBN 0 75430 394 2

FOREWORD

This year, the Poetry Now Young Writers' Kaleidoscope competition proudly presents the best poetic contributions from over 32,000 up-and-coming writers nationwide.

Successful in continuing our aim of promoting writing and creativity in children, each regional anthology displays the inventive and original writing talents of 11-18 year old poets. Imaginative, thoughtful, often humorous, *Kaleidoscope Chester* provides a captivating insight into the issues and opinions important to today's young generation.

The task of editing inevitably proved challenging, but was nevertheless enjoyable thanks to the quality of entries received. The thought, effort and hard work put into each poem impressed and inspired us all. We hope you are as pleased as we are with the final result and that you continue to enjoy *Kaleidoscope Chester* for years to come.

CONTENTS

The Poems

LIMERICK

There was a young man named Tom
Who liked to play football in Brom
He kicked it so high that it reached the sky
That skilful young man called Tom.

Thomas Reeves (11)

MY HELPER

I keep telling her to buy
Modern, fashionable stuff.
But she spends money
On boring stuff.
You can't have
A fashionable conversation with her.
I think my helper has been
On this planet before.
She takes after my Grandma,
Or my Nana's friend.
She listens to old-fashioned music.
Quiche must be old-fashioned
Because she eats it
At Wendy's every Tuesday.
Jean and the school sec. see eye to eye
About everything old-fashioned
Because they are both old.
She's one of them people
That make you do everything.
One mean person.
She's always on holiday,
At home more than she's at work.
Her brain doesn't work.
When she was off one day she didn't tell me
And she calls herself a good helper.
You can't get the staff.
I don't ask her which lesson I'm going to.
She has to ask me because her memory's going.
Jean -
She's my special friend.

Celyn Lea (14)

MY DOG

My dog is silly.
She likes to play ball.
She likes playing with you.
She loves chocolate cake.
She chases cats, tractors
and her friends.
She runs in the house
With her muddy paws.
And Mum shouts,
'Get that dog out.'
She's bonkers!

Liz Waite (16)

IT'S

It's raining
It's cold
It's freezing
It's snowy
It's dark
It's frosty
It's grey
It's foggy
It's awful
It's winter!

Hayley Williams (16)

MY BROTHERS

My brothers are always
Joking with me.
They make me laugh.
They let me
Hear their music.
I like it. It's loud.
They phone me once a month.
They tell me their news.
They send postcards
When on holiday in
Tunisia
My brothers, they love me.

Alicia Gough (14)

MY DAD

I like my Dad
He makes me laugh
When he tickles me.
He makes me laugh
When he pushes me outside.
He brings me nice things from work.
He brings me chocolate.
He is brown and has black hair.
He lives with me all the time.
He carries me upstairs.
If I'm naughty,
He shouts at me.
I shout, 'Dad, I'm sorry.'

Gemma Drury (15)

BARNEY

Barney is my rabbit.
Barney makes me smile.
He's black and white
Lives in a hutch in the garden.
Barney sits on my knee.
Sometimes leaves a mess.
Barney eats plants in the garden.
Makes Mum and Dad shout.
This makes him annoyed.
He runs crazily about.
Barney is big and scary
Fat and ugly.
He has smooth, long hair.
He's stupid but great.
That's Barney.

Katie Gerrard (16)

A DEVOURING DAY

Beat quickly your selected books,
Season with PE kit and pencil case.
Transfer quickly to a pre-heated high school,
And sweat for 15 minutes in assembly.
Simmer in first lesson with Mrs Brameld,
Where a bit of French dressing should be added.
Beat in a circle for 2nd lesson in PE,
Until you can't do it any more.
Season lightly in break with prawn cocktail crisps.
Garnish in geography,
With a bit of continental flavour.
Bake at lunch for a fully risen centre.
Sprinkle with a handful of
Simultaneous equations in Maths.
Then for the finale flambé in Science,
With a nice mixture of juices.
Finally finish off in a relaxed environment,
Where it can be served with 'Neighbours'.

Jack Ritchie (15)

SPRING SNOWDROPS

Two snowdrops snug in their beds
Jack Frost said, 'They're dead.'
'No, no,' said the sun 'they're not dead.'
'Then prove it,' said Jack Frost
'OK,' said the sun.
Then slowly Jack Frost melted away
The snowdrops came that day.

Emma Wilson (11)

WAR

I hear excited laughs, you hear terrifying bangs
I see beautiful birds, you see ugly planes
I feel warm sunshine, you feel blazing fire
I touch wonderful air, you touch terrible death
If I had the choice I would give you my wonderful life
So let's stop those petrifying bangs
Let's stop those disastrous planes
Let's stop those raging fires
And let's stop death.

Charis Holton (12)

SCHOOL RECIPE

Add 600 children to the streets
Defrost until limp and ready to be worked with
Put them in school until boiling point
Let simmer for five separate hours
Then release for 14 and 30 minute breaks
Add extra fillings to body
Then release back into the streets
Put in front of TV
Until mind freezes
Then lay in bed at 10.30
For a good rest.

Richard Thistlewood (15)

How To Make School Pie

Take 600 pupils (preferably early for best results).
Baste with green sweaters and black trousers
And garnish with black shoes or trainers.
Allow enough time to cook until
Ready to be put into school.
Simmer over teachers,
Take out after three hours and turn over.
Replace for another two hours then serve
With a lot of homework
After allowing to cool in front of TV.

Jerome N Burch (15)

Daily Kingsway Recipe

Take 600 large teaspoons of children
put them in a school,
Add 41 teachers and whisk quickly.

Divide the mixture into separate rooms,
leave to warm for about 10 minutes,
Then take off the boil and pour into assembly.

After that separate into three one hour periods,
And leave them to stew.
Then take them out of the ovens,
for dinner for approximately 1 hour.

After that separate again into 2 one hour
periods,
And place them back into the ovens.
Once ready take out of ovens and let them go
home.

Tom Hughes (15)

MOVE ON
OR FRIENDLY ADVICE

Forget about love it's over,
You're never gonna get the girl,
Set your sights on something else,
And see what the future will unfurl.

You've got a brain,
So why don't you use it?
Don't let your heart decide,
Even though you get the feeling,
That your world is being torn apart inside.

Watch her go,
Just let it happen,
To her it'll never feel right,
It's time to move on now,
Let the tears wash her from your sight.

Just listen to what others say,
For her you'd be far too good,
Besides she always got the wrong idea,
And you were always,
Misunderstood..

So look towards the new dawn.
Things will be better this way,
I'm told,
Your heart is young and free now,
Just see what the future holds.

Paul Linfield (16)

WHY SHOULD I LET HER?

Why should I let her rule my life?
Why should I live by her rules?
Can't I have my own life?

Why can't I talk to my friends?
Why do I always have to be with her?
Can't I have friends?

Why shouldn't I go to university?
Why shouldn't I work hard on school work?
Can't I do what I want with my life?

Why must I always say sorry for things I haven't done?
Why should I apologise for things long gone?
Can't I do anything right?

Why can't I go and see my family?
Can't she handle a month without me?
Why can't I see these people I love?

Why is all this happening?
Because in three words I signed my life away.
I said,
'I love you!'

Constantine George Soulounias (16)

WHEN I AM OLD?

When I am old I will wear my old laddered tights under my short skirts
and trainers and get my body tattooed from head to toe.

When I am old I will dye my hair bright red with blue stripes
I will give my grandchildren lots and lots of toys and live in a council
house.

When I am old I will sit at my gate and let children dip in my sweet bag
and make sure they always pull out a scary insect.
When I am old I will wear my old laddered tights.

When I am old I will wear my old laddered tights.

Lucy Burcham (11)

SUSIE

The worst Friday of my life
Never to see her again,
Inside I could hear her name 'Susie'
At dinner I found out,
My mouth tastes like salt,
My heart broke in two,
Her fur so soft,
With a rose in her box where
she lies.

Melissa Townley (13)

BULLY POEM

Dread,
humiliation, pain,
annoyance, intimidation, fury,
helplessness, terror, hatred, isolation,
irritation, aggravation, torture,
misery, harassment,
taunting.

Sam Chadwick (12)

GREECE

There are hills all around
A sound of crickets clicking constantly
And a smell of food drifting around in the arid air.

I can still taste the juices from the lusciously cooked meat
The lights from the restaurant glaring into the night
Attracting every mosquito in Greece like a magnet for feeding time.

The next day we stroll to the beach
My sister clutching her hat and glasses
The glare of the sun magnifying her hangover
She does her daily ritual,
Of lying on the beach till dusk is upon us
Then it's time to start over.

Christopher Cody (13)

WHEN I AM OLD

When I am old I'm going to . . .
Climb hills in the day
Leaving time to go and play
Go to discos and rave all night
Watch the greatest ever fight.

When I am old . . .
I want to wear the latest fashion
Eat sweet things with all my passion
Buy the latest CD's
Climb up all the fully grown trees.

When I am old . . .
I will feast upon the most luscious foods
While watching Liverpool getting booed
There is never a dull moment
Even when I'm in the tent.

When I am old . . .

I don't want to be like a normal old lady
I just want to be
Me!

Rebecca Rollings (11)

TEARS OF AN ONION

Locked away in the dark,
Waiting for the light to come on,
Praying it won't be me,
Hoping the moment won't come.

Suddenly, the door opens,
the light comes on.
She picks me up in her murderous hands
Put me down, let me go.

She places me down,
On a cold hard board
I see the glimmer of her weapon,
The knife raised above me.

She starts to peel away my skin,
Can't she see my tears.
Skinned alive
What a way to go.

She's crying, does she feel guilty?
It's not too late for her to stop.
She doesn't have to chop me up,
And throw me in the pot.

Rebecca Walsh (15)

THE DRAGON UNDER MY BED

Under my bed, I used to think
A dragon was under there.
Whoever went under my bed
Would feel his sharp breath about their knees
His trembling whiskers tickle so,
They squeak and squeal till he lets go.
I hear his far from friendly roar
I see his eyeballs in the dark
Shining in their sockets
As round and big as pears in pockets.
I see his nostrils flaming wide,
His tapering teeth, his jutting jaws
His tongue, his tail, his twenty claws.
His hairy shadow in the moon.
The Dragon suspends pursuit
On the fallen teddies
And while I lie in bed the fierce dragon
Toys, not boys, his talons pierce
With a thumping heart I hear him munch
Six toys at a time he'll crunch
At length he went to sleep and so did I.

Emma Williams (11)

BIRMINGHAM SMALL HEATH

Birmingham, Small Heath.

Light in day darkness at night:
Rain, wind, in misty grey clouds.
Cars on the road going *'Boom Boom!'* smell of petrol dizzy, drizzly;
as black fumes blow in the blue air.
Passing by old chip shop, sweets, candy, food effects my senses,
Smoke of coffee coming from the café, clinching. clutching.
On the brick wall visitors talking, children crying, group of skinheads
screaming, police men shouting.

Birmingham Small Heath, a busy city.

Rabina Ali (14)

WINTER WONDERLAND

The snow it falls tumbling and whirling
Not a care in the world
Spiralling on to the leaves
Unfurled.

Around it goes
Around and around
With
Not a care in the world
It snows.

Me? I'm not bothered
With the cold outside
I'm all snuggled up
In my winter hide.

The decorations up,
The tree aglow
What a wonderful thing
To watch the snow.

Soon it is time
To go to bed
To rest my weary
Little head.

When I wake up at
The crack of dawn
What beholds me
This great morn
A host of gifts
For you and me
And a glorious day
Of festivity.

Natalie Pierce-Jones (11)

DAILY KINGSWAY RECIPE

Fold back curtains,
Prepare and water down
Add mixture of teachers
and students for right consistency.
Sift, sieve and sort through books
knead brains for two hours.
Set time 11.00.
Wrap up ready to cool. Transfer and
simmer for another hour then pour
out and stuff with optional filling.
Place to cook for 2 hours then take
out and place at home, putting mixture
in front of TV, allowing not to rise until morning.

Laura Higgins (15)

❧

SCHOOL RECIPE
(Makes approx 1500)

Whisk up at 7.30,
Rinse well before adding dressing.
Pipe into a school bus,
And simmer for at least 20 minutes.
Transfer to a large school building.

Roll out children into groups of about 30,
Place in lessons.
They should now be boiled for 60 minutes,
Or until very hot.

At 12.30 allow time to settle and marinade.
After 50 minutes shake back into lessons,
Mix well.

When buzzer sounds remove and return to bus.
Simmer for another 20-25 minutes.
Drain and place the mixture in front of
homework.
After approximately 1 hour place in front of
Neighbours.

At 10.30 tip gently into bed for 8 hours.
Repeat for the next four days.

Katie Edge (15)

Daily Kingsway Recipe

Shake several hundred students out of bed and rinse in clean cold water,
Stuff with cereal and toast then wrap in green sweatshirts,
Deliver to school for twenty to nine and allow to cool in form rooms.
Mix different years and forms in a large assembly hall then
Separate pupils into specific classes and allow to roast until break.
For 15 minutes mix friends together and give them time to settle,
At twenty past eleven replace students in their classes
Add one teacher and leave for an hour till lunch.
Whisk them thoroughly for the next 60 minutes
Then return to the classrooms to simmer.
Set timer for half past three then release pupils to their homes,
Allow an entire evening for students to relax until they have to rise
again.

Nicola Macey (15)

MY DAILY RECIPE

My day starts with a pinch of agony and a sprinkle of despair,
I arrive at school with a drop of hope but it soon evaporates.
I am gradually brought to the boil until dinner,
Where glazed relief is brought and I am left to cool.
After dinner it's back to face more simmering teachers,
But at half three a dash of delight is added to my day as I can leave for
home.
Once home, the day rolls out nicely,
Add a drop of tiredness and season with homework and my day is
complete.

Stuart Millard (15)

A DAILY SCHOOL RECIPE

Sprinkle a handful of teachers
not needed to be the finest,
into a very large school.
Take a pinch of ten subjects
and tip in some more.
Leave students in for six hours,
then pour out soon as finished.
When cooled place into homes
carefully rolled in homework,
and add in ten more books.
After two hours in room,
allow time to settle
in front of television screen.
Soon as cooled may be served with
darkness and dipped in bed.

Fu Wing Yip (15)

❦

WHAT IS PAIN

Pain is a tree in summer,
after a day of children swinging and climbing,
it's left its branches and leaves,
flung at the base of its trunk.

After a summer of torture,
children breaking the branches
it stands cold, alone nursing its wounds;
baring its soul to the world.

In winter the tree stands
bare and uncomfortable
thrashing from side to side,
its gnarled bark twisted, graffitied
showing the scars of a tortuous summer.

In spring time it weeps,
crying out fresh life,
forcing leaves through
its once barren branches,
for what? To be tortured once again!

Richard Daly (16)

HATE IS A BIN

My hollowness echoed.
Empty.
Used.
The bin sat silently
Hallow
Wasteful
The same as my hatred.
Somehow it looked smaller
My mind grew narrower
Focusing on the bin
Suddenly my hatred became overwhelming
Out of control.
I shouted and cursed
The bin was rolling
Unstoppable.
Now it sits silent and hollow again
Mulling
Waiting innocently, before
It topples and is out of control
Once more.

Philip Dutton (16)

WINDOW PAIN

People see through pain with ease
And forget the glass which separates two sides
They just look out, ignoring the hurt . . .
No one sees the hand prints
That put pressure on the weakest part.

The fact that the frame is broken
And hurts more and more each day
Is inconsequential to all
The paint flakes, the frame breaks
And if not tended to will worsen . . .

Allowing the window to fall and shatter
Into one thousand tiny pieces
Leaving a large hollow space
Which used to be pain's shelter
But is now just a void.

Caris Williams (16)

JEALOUSY IS MY ROCKING CHAIR

Jealousy hurts like the splintered oak of an old rocking chair.
It stays hidden under a blanket of security,
in a large empty space forgotten by everyone but me.
Never balanced, forever swaying,
like the rocking emotions from hatred to love.
I ache inside, I've been bitten by jealousy,
like the rotting, termite infected wood,
which is slowly broken down by the changing of the seasons.
I take a deep breath letting out my frustration,
and smell the deception in the air.
It smells like the must of that large empty space,
and hurts like the splinters of an old rocking chair.

Phil Morgan (16)

MONTHS OF THE YEAR

January brings the cold,
especially felt by the old.
February short and sweet,
with Valentine's Day and chocolates to eat.
March is the start of spring,
which brings flowers and everything.
April is Easter time,
I put my eggs in a line.
May is the Cup Final at Wembley,
it's a very exciting time for me.
June is the month when I was born,
we have a party on the lawn.
July is when it should be hot,
but it very often rains a lot.
August we have the whole month off school,
which I think is really cool!
September back to school we go,
in whose class we do not know.
October brings Hallowe'en,
pumpkins and conkers are to be seen.
November brings us Bonfire night,
the fireworks set the sky alight.
In December we decorate the Christmas tree
which is great fun for you and me.

Daniel Underhill (11)

ME

When I was one I started to crawl.
When I was two I started to walk.
When I was three I started to talk.
When I was four I started to talk better.
When I was five I started to dress myself.
When I was six I started to feed myself.
When I was seven I started to read.
When I was eight I started to write better.
When I was nine I started to ride a bike.
When I was ten I was a year five at Newton School.
Now I am eleven I am at Kingsway High School.

Hayley Sutcliffe (11)

MY FAVOURITE THINGS

James Bellinger is my name
I hope one day I'll be covered in fame
I was born on April 2nd 1987
Which makes me now aged eleven

I am me
That's all I can be
Football's the theme
Tottenham's my team
My favourite player's Sol Campbell
He gives the strikers real hell
By stopping them from scoring
And the scoreboard soaring

Computer games are things I like
But not ones where you have a fight
Football and strategy games are what I like to see
The kind of games that suit me.

James Bellinger (11)

WHEN I WAS LITTLE

When I was little,
I was scared of the dark
A monster lived under my bed
The shadows were monsters
That grabbed me all night

When I was little
Dark shadows were scary
I couldn't get out of my bed
'Cause of the hand that would grab my leg

When I was little
I was scared of my mum
Coming into my room
She turned into a monster or something like that

But mum could scare them away
With a flick of the light I found out what the monsters were
The teddies were monsters
The cat was the hand or paw from under the bed

When I was little, when I was tiny
I was scared of the dark
I'm not scared any more.

Honest?

Ygraine Hinton (11)

THE FUTURE

Do you ever wonder
What the future will be like?
Boys could be called Tina
Girls could be called Mike
Dogs could be cats
Cats could be dogs
Do you ever wonder
What the future will be like?
Light could be darkness
Darkness could be light
Our heads could be balls
Ducks as walls
I don't care
What happens to the squeak and the baa
I just want it to stay as it is
But just imagine, are heads as balls
Do you ever wonder
What the future will be like
The beep and the bite
Do you ever wonder?

Karen Langford (11)

MY WINDOW LEDGE

Sitting on my window ledge,
I wonder what gifts life will bring,
Good or bad.
I wait to live, I wait to die,
I wait for some other option.
Life is special,
I don't intend to waste it.
Things come as they come,
I have to accept it.
That's life from my window.

Stephanie Shephard (12)

NO-MAN'S-LAND

A dream,
a wish,
to never come true.
Happiness for me and you
but then it's back to the real world,
life on earth, how absurd.
How could anything be so cold
to turn its back on new and old.
Smiles and laughter is what joy brings,
if you haven't got it, you are sinned.
For people who live in no-man's-land,
love and laughter is completely banned.

Amy Dennan (11)

KINGSWAY RECIPE

Measure out 600 pupils,
And pour into empty school,
Making sure all pupils are scrapped out of bed.
Fold in books,
Separate mixture into each classroom,
And stuff with education.
Once stuffed, fry with a pinch of homework,
Then, leave to simmer at home,
Until next morning.

Katie Barlow (15)

SCHOOL RECIPE

Step 1 - Pour precisely out of bed, into school.

Step 2 - Stir carefully all the pupils.

Step 3 - Add noise, teachers and discipline.

Step 4 - Place children in different rooms.

Step 5 - After 3 hours of work separate.

Step 6 - Sprinkle some fun, add a teaspoon of laughter.

Step 7 - Whip wildly for 10 minutes.

Step 8 - Put into classrooms 'til golden.

Step 9 - Remove from school to cool down.

Step 10 - Place in front of the TV.

Step 11 - After the meal serve homework.

Step 12 - When ready deeply dip into bed.

Danielle Hartles (15)

Hate Is A Table
(Carvings on an old school desk)

Hate is a table,
Clothed in lies,
Covered with other people's secrets,
Condemned to detest,
All abstract and scarred,
Covered to ignore its disgust,
At people's repulsion to others.

> Hate is a table,
> Etched in untruths,
> Cruelly smothered in feeble excuses
> Made to accept the bitter word of many,
> Forced to bear people's grudges,
> Engraved with ill wishes,
> Deep incisions wounding its face.

Rachel Nickless (16)

Daily Kingsway Recipe

Prepare equipment night before.
After 8 hours covered, uncover and allow to rise.
Scrub until clean and add garnish.

At 9.00 am fill one hall lined with chairs until full and
follow information.
Pipe out sentences onto paper for 3 hours, until time to add filling.

Return to simmer for a further 2¼ hours,
before turning out at 3.30 pm.

Transfer to dry place and relax in front of TV.

Around 10.30 pm place in fridge, close door and off goes light
until next day.

Maybe served with matching uniform for each pupil,
consisting of green sweatshirts and white shirt.

Michelle Kozlowski (16)

KINGSWAY'S INGREDIENTS

Take one teenager
and leave to marinade in
bed for at least 8 hours.
Take out and leave alone for
half an hour. Stuff with breakfast
then wrap in green jumper. Transport
it to school and mix with other
ingredients. Season with maths, English
and science, and heat up in PE. Once
boiling, leave to simmer for a further
two hours, before removing from school.
Leave to cool for an hour, laying
it flat, after which, peeling off
the uniform. Poach in hot water
and drain off excess. Leave
to settle before lining in
pyjamas and carefully pouring
into bed. Decorate with a
sprig of homework if
desired.

Beverley Fletcher (16)

READING BETWEEN THE LINES

Interesting cover attracts the eye,
deserving more than a passing glance.
Introduction may suggest a hint of true romance.

Imagination captured, opening to appeal.
First impressions positive, yet more to be revealed.

I want to spend my time with you
and get to know you better,
the nature of your character,
to the very letter.

I feel that now I know you,
no longer a closed book.
Doting on your every word,
since off the shelf I took.

Daniel Gray (16)

KINGSWAY RECIPE

Scoop 600 surly teenagers from bed and mix with green vegetables.
Divide into groups and place in classrooms.
Mix them together every hour as you transfer them from room to room.
Place all pupils in a large room and sprinkle with chips.
Again, let them glaze before numerous flames
and after simmering all day, transfer them to their own homes.
Allow to cool for a couple of hours, before placing in
own beds and folding over their blankets.
To be served with books and pens.

Kimberley Bate (15)

DAILY KINGSWAY RECIPE

Open doors and funnel in kids.
Filter into separate rooms.

Take a third and leave to simmer in assembly.
Add glazed head teacher to help strain.

Sprinkle slowly to lessons.
Place in warm room with radiator on
and windows closed and leave to boil.

Allow time to wilt before moving
to different lessons.

Do this five times in total,
by the fifth time they will
noticeably rise.

Move to tutor room where,
in under two minutes they
will start to expand from the
centre slowly.

Open doors and serve into
different houses.

Adam Linfield (15)

THE DAILY KINGSWAY RECIPE

Collect together about 600 moaning, tired students,
Add 39 grumpy, preoccupied teachers and 2 pregnant hormone-raging women,
Mix together for 5 minutes, then separate into three bowls,
Clearly marking them: Northgate, Watergate and Eastgate.
Disperse to several containers, and leave to learn for 1 hour,
Mix together in a narrow and long baking tin, add cheap and vulgar paint that clashes for colour,
Separate for one hour and settle.
Blend together and add a hatch, screaming teens, and a dining room full of year 11s.
Toss in empty cans, packets, wrappers and leftover flaky pastry from sausage rolls.
Stir in a helping of drama and bring to the boil.
Mix in a dinner queue, pushes and shoves, pour in Mrs Griffiths and knead into a single strand.
Cover for 55 minutes, no longer!
Whisk for five minutes and fold in two measures of maths and lighten with giggles and sad jokes.
Other optional ingredients are: marinated Shakespeare, calculators and test tube and T-charts, detentions and catch-up sessions.
If you have not followed the recipe correctly, you must simmer for an extra 10 minutes.
This recipe should be served with white shirts, black trousers or skirts and green jumpers,
If anything froths over, for example, shirts, it must be put back in.
So wait until 3.30, serve and enjoy!

Katie Johnson (15)

ALTON TOWERS

Alton Towers is full of screaming
echoing from the ride.
The touch of money when you're in the shop.
'I want it' a little boy cried.
The click as the big rides start
and more screaming when the rides dip.
The dreaded sight of the mile long queues.
It's up and down on the ship.

Liam Dalton (13)

The KWH Recipe

Remove children and teachers from beds,
Place with care into Kingsway High School,
Mix together teachers and children,
After three hours gently separate and leave to simmer,
Sieve together again for two hours,
Cut apart using fish slice and allow to go home,
Stir children carefully with homework,
When complete leave to boil in front of the telly,
Then immerse with skewer in a warm bed,
Repeat this process five days a week,
Within five years with difficult preparation
a surprising result will appear.

Fiona Gunn-Jackman (15)

DAILY KINGSWAY RECIPE

Take as many children as you can.
Tip into large building and liquidize.
Fold in a handful of teachers,
And leave in a warm classroom,
To rise for two hours.
Strain the mixture and leave
To marinate for fifteen minutes
In place of own choice.
When settled, bake in hot oven,
Then stuff with bits of food before
Grilling gently, being careful not to
Over heat - the mixture could erupt.
Tip out of building and finely chop.
Leave to cool before consumption.

Keith Oakley (16)

BONFIRE

Glowing, the bonfire is starting.
Flickering, the sparks fly.
Starting, but not yet burning.
Growing, timidly it comes into life.

Burning, with bright orange flames.
Roaring, bright and very hot.
Dancing, high in the sky.
Shouting, full of joy.

Smouldering, lots more smoke.
Fading, the flames die down.
Shrinking, becoming smaller and smaller.
Trying, to find its soul.

Lying, the flames are dying.
Resting, only the ashes in sight.
Decaying, no one sees to it.
Leaving, everyone has gone.

Jennifer Crich (13)

AUTUMN

Golden leaves and dragonflies,
The smell of Mum's home-made apple pies,
The warm gentle autumn breeze,
Blows away lots of red-brown leaves.

In the park children stamping on crisp, crunchy leaves,
'We're having so much fun we don't want to leave,'
Mushrooms and fungi appear from the ground,
But toadstools and stinkhorns are nowhere to be found.

Icicles are appearing, Jack Frost is here,
Run away squirrels for winter is here.

Leonora Russell (11)

I'D LIKE TO BE A BRIDESMAID...

I'd like to be a bridesmaid,
To dress in pink and white,
I'd get to go to a party
And stay up all night!

I'd be in lots of photos,
People would stop and stare,
They'd look at me and the other bridesmaids
And say how lovely we were.

I'd be given lots of presents,
Hugs and kisses too!
I'd love to be a bridesmaid,
'Can I be one for you?'

Laura Jane Evans (11)

THE MARRIAGE

It was the day my sister was going to marry
A man called Charles Frederick Barry.
She wore the most beautiful dress
And so did I, and her best friend Tess.

We were the bridesmaids, as you can see,
We had bouquets of flowers, Tess and me.
But my sister got one which was bigger -
She hummed a song, I sang with vigour.

We got to the church, traditionally late,
And met Mrs Barry, née Tate,
Who said to my sister Joy,
Mind you treat him good, my boy.

The music started, we walked down the aisle,
We went so slowly, it felt like a mile.
He was wearing a flower - oh no, not a poppy!
They grinned at each other - yuck! - how soppy!

The vows were over, the work was done,
Everyone was beaming - bright as the sun.
Off they went on their honeymoon,
It's a pity they're going to be back so soon.

Antonia Parker (11)

WHAT A FUSS!

Crawling, scrambling, sprawling,
Right across the floor,
Dribbling, gargling, gurgling,
Wandering round, trying to explore.

Yes, I'm talking about babies,
Plump, chubby and round,
Teetering and tottering, bawling and screaming,
What a dreadful sound.

Babbling, murmuring, shouting,
They do the most extraordinary things,
Pretending to be an elephant,
Pretending they have wings.

Slurping their drink, playing with their food,
Their eating manners are poor,
Milk on the table, peas in their ears,
Custard trickling down the door.

Walks in the pram, rides in the car,
Desperate to get them to sleep,
Then they're woken by lorries clanging by,
Or car horns going beep, beep!

They scribble on walks,
They tread on the cat,
They break all their toys,
They take your new hat.

You take them out, they make a fuss,
They scream and wail and shout,
They want to be fed, they want to go home,
They desperately want to get out.

But they're just babies, they're only new,
So give them a chance to show what they can do.

Kathryn Wright (10)

OCEAN SONG

The ocean is alive
With sound -
Ocean sound

Songs of dancing
Waves playing
Rolling, crashing
down -
Ocean sound

Songs of celebration
Dolphins, whales
and fish -
Ocean sound

Songs of joy
Shoals of fish
a leaping -
Ocean sound

Songs of nature
Coloured coral
Growing -
Ocean sound

Songs of legends
Mermaids great
Sea monsters -
Ocean sound

Songs that have
no end, bottomless
depths -
Ocean sound

Voices beyond
the ear of man -
Ocean sound

Ocean song.

Victoria Tudor-Jones (11)

MY FAMILY

My mum is a collector -
The house is always filled with junk.
My dad's a school inspector -
He doesn't like me being a punk!

My sister spends her life on the phone,
We always have a mile long bill.
My grandma spends her day at home,
Thinking of new things to put in her will!

My two cats love to play,
Then lie full stretch in the warm sun.
My grandad works in the garden all day,
There's lots of jobs that must be done.

Sophie Patrick (11)

CATS

Tabby cats prowling, stalking their prey,
Siamese practising their song every day.
Cheetahs having their daily jog,
A lion eating a warthog.

There is a Manx without his tail,
And Burmese cats with their long wail.
The leopard with his big black spots,
Cats eat mice, yes lots and lots.

Cats hiding in the undergrowth,
They climb as well as a sloth.
To the heavens they sing,
To the bark they cling.

Running here, dodging there,
Dogs can't find them anywhere!
Tortoise shells basking in the sun,
Many rosettes this cat has won.

Emma Swe (11)

EXTINCTION

H er silver hide glinted and shone,
U pon her platter, bones there were none,
N evertheless, flesh she did eat,
T itbits of meat stuck between her teeth,
E xtinct, is soon a word that will describe her race,
D riven from the world and all space.

B luey-grey ice is her only bed,
E xhausted, she laid down her head,
A part from the spider that's crawled up the wall,
S olitary confinement was the only call,
T races of her have never been found, none at all,
   Or have there?

Vicky Hughes (11)

AUTUMN

The freshness of a new day,
The cold crisp breeze,
The crunching carpet of leaves,
The robin red-breast whistling by,
The rustling of the squirrels in the trees,
The dying sun in the sky,
The drops of dew from a morning mist,
The birds flying by, travelling to far off lands,
The autumn clothes in the shops,
The small insects looking for a home,
The squirrels collecting for a winter's sleep,
The polished conkers falling off the trees,
The orange and yellow leaves on the trees,
The leaf patterns of falling leaves,
The early sunsets in the sky,
The exciting autumn bonfire nights!

Joanne Mia Cornes (11)

THE WORST MATHS LESSON IN HISTORY!

Our maths teacher's name is Sue,
You don't know what she makes us do.
Fifty sums all in a row,
We sit here thinking 'I don't know.'
3 + 3 and 6 + 4,
Two pupils faint upon the floor.
'What's 12 + 5?' she said to me,
The fainted pupils rose to three.
Four more children began to swoon,
We'd all be down before it got to noon!
One by one the others fell,
I wondered 'Will I hear the bell?'
'What's 9 x 5?' I heard Sue say,
'Oh no' I thought as I passed away.

Sarah Sweeney (11)

WHAT IS YOUR NAME?

What is your name?
Is it Jane or is it Jenny or Jo?
Oh please tell me, I need to know.
Don't go, I need to know.

Is it Emily or Katy or Hatty?
No, no, don't go, I've nearly got it.
Oh I've got it, it's Sally isn't it.
No, no, it's not that.

Is it Sophie, Susan or Sian?
Please don't leave,
I think I've nearly got it.
Oh I know, it begins with A.
Is it Alexandra, Antonia or Andrea?

I remember it's Victoria.
No, no, it's Tessa or Tasmin or Teresa.
No, I don't think it's any of those.
Oh I know, it's Charlotte or Carol.

Oh please don't go, I need to know.
I'm sorry I've got it wrong,
But what is your name?
It's Jack?
Oh, you're a boy!

Alice Mason (11)

THE CAT

The cat, black as midnight,
fur shining and gleaming like a star,
creeping through the city at night,
through a dark alley with dustbins either side
and the light of passing cars, people's houses
and street lights flooding the narrow entrance.
A dustbin clatters to the ground,
spilling rubbish onto the concrete.
The cat backs away hissing at a snarling dog.
He turns and trots back through the alley,
flickering his ebony tail.
He walks his slow, calm walk into the street
of dazzling and flashing lights,
and the sound of cars, car radio music, shouting, laughing and
talking and clubs all mix together into a confusing noise.
He makes a dash across the road, while cars screech to a halt
all around him.
He slinks off into another alley, but a familiar one.
He steps through a familiar cat flap where a familiar voice says
'Hello puss. Ready for your dinner?'

Sioned Jones (11)

SPIDERS OF THE BELFRY

The cool morning sun makes us shiver,
It makes our webs shine and glitter.
We look up at the sky and there beyond,
Where the fire rages on.
The fire of London spreads as we speak,
And grabs small children mild and meek.
And flames of silver turn to gold,
And emerald dragons, birds of gold,
Jewelled daggers, wealth untold.
But small old rags and dusty coins,
And all that's precious are burnt and gone.
And as we sit upon our perch,
Higher than the old grey birch,
We close our eyes and softly pray,
As the bells strike two that day.
And all we can do is softly cry,
And watch this evil world go flying by.
We spiders of the belfry.

Helen Fitton (11)

WINTER'S MOON

You shimmer in the sky at night,
And smile from each icy lake,
You whisper dreams while I'm asleep,
And take them when I wake.

This wintertime, you'll light the sky,
Illuminate the snow,
And when the dark clouds block you,
I'll wonder where you go.

When summer arrives this coming year,
It'll shorten your time to play,
I'll try to stay up to watch you,
But you'll slowly drift away.

Gemma Ball (11)

IT'S NEARLY HERE!

Blue cars,
Red cars,
People driving green cars,
Traffic rushing,
Crowds a' pushing,
Midnight's nearly here.

Blue hats,
Red hats,
People wearing green hats,
Echoes calling,
Shadows falling,
Midnight's nearly here.

Blue lights,
Red lights,
Neon flashing green lights,
Streets a' clearing,
Bells a' peeling,
Midnight's nearly here.

Blue trees,
Red trees,
Fairy lights on green trees,
Tinsel shining,
People dining,
Midnight's nearly here.

Blue bows,
Red bows,
Boxes tied with green bows,
Children playing,
People praying,
Christmas day is here.

Deborah Wynn (11)

WEATHER

Pitter-patter goes the rain on the window
like someone trying to get in.

The wind howls all around
like a werewolf crying to the moon.

Lightning flashes in the sky
like a streak of yellow paint.

Thunder bursts from the heavens
like a loud roll of drums.

Clouds speed across the sky
like runners in a race.

The sun lights up the world
like an automatic light.

Mist shrouds the Earth
like a thick, white cloak.

But however powerful all these wonders seem
they all belong to their ruler,

       Mother Nature.

Sarah Bennion (11)

CHRISTMAS

C is for chimney that Santa comes down,
H is for holly that never goes brown,
R is for ribbons that we tie in a bow,
I is for ice that follows the snow,
S is for Santa who delivers the presents,
T is for turkey though some eat pheasants,
M is for Mary the mild kind mother,
A is for angels who care for each other,
S is for stable where Jesus was born.

Danielle Steven (11)

GONE AND COMING

The round fluorescent sun, that shines until nine,
Oh, I wish it was mine.
I would leave it up every year and every day,
Instead of pushing it away.

Oh, summer's gone.

The fresh green leaves are turning a rusty brown,
Soon they will be tumbling down.
The calm blue sky is turning a grumpy grey,
The robin's back, catching prey.

Autumn's nearly here.

Crinkled leaves are slowly, delicately falling,
The little robins are calling.
The still, cold darkness is coming, now knowing,
That daylight's gradually going.

Winter's on its way.

Before you know, we'll have a great tree,
And everyone shouting full of glee.
'Christmas is here at last, Christmas is here.'
Then it will be a brand New Year.

1999 will be here.

Hannah Blaikie (11)

DOLPHINS IN THE SEA

D olphins, dolphins in the sea,
   flicking tails and splashing me.
O ut in the sea the sun shines down,
   glistening on the little town.
L eaping, prancing, jumping high,
   right up where the birds do fly.
P laying, splashing, tail flapping,
   little dolphin is a-clapping.
H e dives down deep,
   from very steep.
I n the water he swims round,
   looking very profound.
N ever scared, not a care in the world,
   just swims round, never hurled.
S afely jumps and leaps up high,
   right up to the blue, blue sky.

I n the water his reflection is there,
   ooh, now it's gone just rippling fair.
N ow underwater the dolphin looks for food,
   he's in a very hungry mood.

T he dolphin sees a fish from the corner of his eye,
   then makes a turn and the fish swims by.
H e comes up again to have a peep,
   then goes back down to have a sleep.
E agerly he looks for a place to sleep,
   ahh, here's a place to keep.

S leepy dolphin goes to sleep,
   zzzz, wakes up in the deep.
E merging from the water's edge.
A nd leaps up high like before in the sky.

Charlotte Elliott (11)

THE MIDNIGHT DANCE FLOOR

It's still, quiet, calm and shiny,
It could be used as a dancing floor,
With people dancing, tiptoeing quietly.
But, when the midnight ball is over,
It shatters against the sandy bay.
Until again, in the middle of the night,
It calms its anger and does not roar,
But flattens its surface to a dancing floor.

Danielle Dykes (12)

BY THE RIVER

Dark, tall lonely trees everywhere.
The smell of fresh flowers spread through the chilly breeze.
Clouds look like familiar faces.
But who am I really?
Where shall my life end?
The stones piled deeply into the lonely earth.
Flowers of every colour reflect through my mind.
Now the river so calm, so peaceful.
Will my life ever be as peaceful as that which lies before my eyes?

Andrea Stephan (11)

ROSE

Alight like a lantern,
Alight with colour,
Breaking away from a budding mother,
Your bud is tight,
Not a wrinkle in sight,
Sway alone on this cold, cold night,
Wilt, wilt, bronzed with age,
Toasted, golden a petal a day,
Your beautiful rose no longer,
Alight no more,
A sadness shared.

Sophie Russell (12)

A POEM ON . . .

I didn't know what kind of poem to write,
One that's funny,
Or one that gives you a fright.
One about teachers, one about friends,
Or one about the world coming to an end.
Should I write in the style of Shakespeare, Wordsworth or Burns,
Maybe one that makes your stomach churn?
Oh dear, this is giving me such grief,
I've got it!
One about the Great Barrier Reef.
To write about noise or boys,
No, I'm too young for that,
Maybe I'll write about spoilt brats.
I could write about illness compare it with health,
What about poverty next to such wealth?
What about nursery rhymes like Jack and Jill?
But for me it would be nagging teachers rolling down the hill.
Shall I write about death in this world,
Or life in the next?
What about a poem that doesn't rhyme?
Yes I like the sound of that.
What about chocolate?
What about sweets?
What about the candy maker who lives down the street?
What about children who are sweet and kind?
And what about parents who have lost their minds?
To write about day, night or noon.
I've got it! I've written a poem for you.
But I'd better end it quick,
Because I need the loo!

Fiona A Middleton (12)

ESCAPING THE CANVAS

(This poem is about a painting of a storm by Turner)

A tsunami of dashing oils,
Proud ship silhouetted against the overcast sky,
Thunderous waves crash across the canvas,
White horses fly over the surf,
Raging torrent tamed by a brush,
And dashed upon the artist's palette,
Swirling into a fury,
Then softened by a dab of turpentine,
Artist's passion fuels the boat,
A cyclone spun with paint.
A crescendo of gushing foam,
Sea meets sky with no horizon,
Breaking the boundary between canvas and reality.

Cassandra Campbell (12)

THE HUNTED AND THE HUNTER

Ears alert like radar receivers,
head still as a doll.
Hind legs stiff and waiting
waiting for the hunter's gun.

He tramples through the thorny bush
awaiting for a catch.
His gun at his side all ready and set,
Set for a rabbit, hare or mouse.

The sound of a *bang* from a rifle sounds,
he flees like a racer on the starting whistle.
Agile, slender, sprinting across the turf
no turning back for an anxious look
looking to see if he'll make it.

He shoots with a shudder,
the anxiety's strong.
With no tea in his pocket can he go home?
But, he's a huntsman, brave and hard,
hard to survive on this food very long.

He ducks under a bush,
the familiar smell.
Of his warren, he's survived.
All is well.

A sense of dread, the food got away
but in the corner a tall slim bird.
Bang! The prize is earned.

Heather Rees (12)

PAST AND PRESENT . . .

An old quiet farmhouse surrounded by trees
That are swaying gently in the morning breeze.
The cry of a cockerel breaks the peace
As does the loud honking of a gaggle of geese.
A gentle brown cow chewing its cud,
The wallowing of pigs in the thick, brown mud.
The rustle of reeds as the coot swims by,
The dapple-grey cart horse lets out a sigh.
The tiny squirrels running on the lawn.
In the woods nearby, there is a brand new fawn,
A hedgehog rustling in the new-found leaves
While passing a hive, the sound of bees.

This is the beginning of a 'past' day . . .

Air, full of hot smelly car fumes.
Big black cloud over the city looms.
Crisp packets, coke cans cover the street,
Newspapers, cigarette ends dirty the park seat.
Tarmaced roads going nowhere.
Orphaned children sleeping on tangled hair.
Sellers shouting out sale, on sale!
In a rich man's house, bread's going stale
While poor people beg with nothing to eat.
Do we really care who's sleeping on the street?
Women shop with small brown bags,
Soon to be stolen by the child in rags.

This is the beginning of a 'present' day . . .

We are a mixture of both of these -
Can't we keep it the 'past' way, please!

Sarah Rivers (12)

THE DOLPHINS' STORY

In the beginning there was the sea
endless peace, tranquillity.

The land creatures lived and on land they died
but the sea loved us and took us inside.
And so we lived 'neath the emerald spray
adapting, evolving, day by day.
We made our own language and used it with glee.
We were happy together, just us and the sea.

But soon it all changed, man thought he knew best
he rescued some creatures and killed all the rest.
Destroying the land and polluting our sea
we lay low and waited how bad could he be?

And so we're still playing and day by day
man is rethinking his troublesome ways.
We tell the old stories, traditions we keep
and show man what fun it is, down in the deep.
We do what we can and have fun in the sea
we've been as helpful as we can be.

The sea is our home and, like an old friend
its love covers everything, it knows no end.
Whatever happens, and when and where
forever and ever . . . the sea will be there.

Laura Bestow (12)

A POEM ABOUT LIFE

Life, what is life?
What is the meaning!

You're born
Screaming, yelling.
Always wanting attention,
But you can't say what
you want . . .

You live.
Get an education,
Get a life
Get a job
And take one day at a time.

You die,
Quietly, peacefully,
Just an old person in bed
one night . . .

Life, what is life?
What is the meaning . . . !

Jacqui Tsang (13)

THE CIRCLE OF SEASONS

September mist is coming
the leaves are on the ground.
Wind is whistling all around
and conkers have fallen without a sound.

Icicles are everywhere
hanging from the gutters.
Even in the sand pits
the golfers bag their putters.

Spring is here at last
hoping that winter has passed.
Flowers are blooming radiantly
covering the ground with a colourful cast.

Summer is here once again
to face the glaring sun.
Filling the countryside with colours,
that to soon will all be done

Kathryn Wilson (13)

SHADOWS OF LIGHT

Trees now whispering shadows,
Still and dark.
Holding secrets of the velvet sky
of the deepest blue.

The ground lies still,
Under a calm black sea.
Hopes and fears are met here,
Beneath this draping veil.

Slow grey light
overtaking the blue.
Faint, but deep inside there's something more,
The power and secrets of the dawn.

The light struggles on,
Slowly emerging,
From the darkest hour.
A pearl in the storm.

A glimmer of red
breaks into the sky.
Hope and life dancing.
Dark years forgotten.

Rich red streaks
race across the sky.
Dawn is here,
Victory has come.

The battle is won . . .

Fiona Stewart (13)

DRIED QUICKLY BY DEATH

Silence, absolute absence of sound,
absence of life,
absence of joyful and happy faces,
absence of everything - except
blackness, sadness, darkness, coldness.
Silence - no longer; cries, sniffs,
coughs to rid of tears, unsuccessfully.
Sounds suddenly dying,
being won over by silence, by death, by darkness.
Faces smothered with streaks of tears,
like streams, but silent, less pleasurable.
Lips buried by cold fingers,
dampened by the rivers of teardrops,
dried quickly by death.
Minds stabbed abruptly by pain,
hit with shock,
left shaking, trembling.
Staring into darkness,
not believing, disbelieving.
Once more, deep silence becomes overruled,
by whispers, by slight movement,
but death, darkness, depression, coldness are stronger,
and any sound is *dried quickly by death.*

Adele Groom (13)

CHOCOLATE

Chocolate, you're brilliant for
congratulations.
Chocolate, you're wonderful for
commiserations.
Chocolate, you have always been there for me.
When I was feeling low you always lifted me.
When I was upset you set my mind straight,
and helped to determine my fate.
When I passed that English test
You made me feel on top of the world.
A mixture of light and dark the chocolate was swirled.
You showed I cared when it came to Easter.
Allowing me to feast on your central mixture.
You never left me on my own,
Without you I would never have grown.
You are the best friend ever.
I will never dislike you.

Oh chocolate! How could I live without you . . . ?

Ruth Watson (13)

A WINTER WONDERLAND

Frosted flakes scatter,
Falling from the sky
On to the surface of the world.
The snow delicately touches the trees
And a brown outline is left.
The fragile carpet of white
Is untouched by the dwellers of the Earth.
And the misty sky,
Blends in with the snowy scene.

An innocent cloud moves,
A glimpse of yellow brightness appears.
It's the sun creeping out from hiding,
It's luminous body beams down brightly on the scene.
The great God is slowly destroying the wonderland.
By tomorrow, this striking, vivid picture
Will be drowned by wetness.
Why do we have to see such a thing
Slowly drifting . . . drifting away!

Elise Hague (13)

A POWDERED OR SOLID FOOD
MADE FROM ROASTED CACAO SEEDS

'It will make you fat!'
'It will give you spots!'
'Eat too much and you'll be sick!'
I don't care what anyone says;
Chocolate is always there for me.

I spent my first morning away from Mum;
No parents, no home and no sister.
Just other children in the same boat as me,
And someone they called the teacher.
But then came the morning break;
And chocolate . . . you were there for me.

When I failed that exam,
When trouble loomed,
When I was ill,
In fact, whenever I needed comfort;
Toffee and fudge cannot deny,
That chocolate . . . you were always be there for me.

My comfort and joy,
My trustworthy friend,
My counsellor and my faithful guide.
I don't care what anyone says;
Chocolate . . . I'll always be there for you!

Samantha Kakati (13)

I'M REALLY SCARED

It's so quiet
I'm on my own
There is nobody around.
Except for a few cobwebs and spiders,
I'm really scared
The silence is really loud so that it's very creepy.
Not even the ring of a telephone or the whistle of the wind.
It's so quiet I could hear a pin drop.
I'm sitting here like a statue.
I'm too scared to move
It's like I'm waiting for something scary to happen.
But I'm not scared anymore.
Because my mum is now home.
I'll be safe now
Mum will protect me
She won't hurt me.
I wasn't scared, honestly!
I was just pretending
But it's not my mum,
I'm really scared
I don't know what to do . . . !

Ruth Cornock (13)

LEFT BEHIND

A solitary figure
stood
looking out at the bleak moors.

Dilapidated frameworks
scattered
the derelict landscape.

Nothing moved
except
the tattered remnants of her clothes.

The wind blew
relentlessly
as it had always done.

Nothing lived
she
was completely alone.

A lone tear
rolled
down her forlorn face.

She remembered
all
that had lived.

For death had taken all
but her
On that cold September night.

Martha Cherry (13)

SUNDAY MORNING

Angelic tones echoing
bright faces sparkling.
A mixture of age, race and gender
hymns on the radio.

Savoury scents floating
oven burning with heat.
Binding vegetables and seasoned meat
the Sunday roast cooking.

Rear wheels gleaming and sparkling
vacuum buzzing away.
Murky water dusting the bonnet
neighbours washing their cars.

Bellies are full and bloated
slumped lazy in the chair.
Unread supplements strewn across the floor,
Sunday evening is here.

Sophie Cookson (13)

THE FIRE AT NUMBER FOUR

People were standing watching in awe,
as the fire burned brightly at number four.
Hoping that someone had rung the brigade
I ran back inside and the noise did fade.

I told my mum, she told my dad,
we went outside and all felt bad.
For all their possessions that they had
had gone in a trace and they would not be glad.

The fire engine then raced down our street,
as everyone began to feel the heat.
The noise increased as the engine drew near
and all the firemen jumped out in their gear.
Hugs then went all around,
and the applause for the fire-fighters made a very loud sound.
The firemen then went on their way,
after having a very successful day.

Emma Graham (13)

YOU ARE...

You are my mother
the one who will build me.
I know there will be no other
for you are always there . . .

As I learn to cope
with the world ahead.
I know holding my rope
you are always there . . .

When I need a friend
one that is true
I know till the end
you are always there . . .

You are my mother
the one who built me.
I know there is no other
you are always there . . .

Rujuta Roplekar (13)

MY SCHOOL DAY

To start we had art where we made masks,
From tissue and PVA glue.
I got papier mâché on my hands,
So I had a pair of gloves too.

And then we had to do gymnastics
(I don't understand what it's for).
Everyone was balanced in pyramids,
But my group fell flat on the floor.

In music we did *ostinatos*
And I had to play the bassoon.
But all of my group got *F minus*
Because I'd forgotten my tune.

At lunch I went into the canteen
I sat down to eat up my soup.
I knocked the whole bowl off the table
So my skirt got covered in gloop.

And then the next lesson was drama
We practised a play by Shakespeare.
In act 2, scene 3 - I fell over
And everyone started to cheer.

In chemistry we did diffusion
Which sounds like a quite simple task.
But I added some copper sulphate
And blew up the conical flask.

We had to write poems in English
I sat down and picked up my pen.
My poem was first-class and funny
That's why I got ten out of ten.

Catriona MacKenzie (13)

THE NEW GIRL

Standing, stooping in the corner of the classroom.
The new girl peered down nervously at her freshly polished,
leather school shoes.
Frozen with fear, she leant silently against the cream wall
while her new classmates, total strangers to her,
either gossiped, sitting in small huddles,
not welcoming intruders, like her - the new girl.
Or hyperactively ran around the room.
Boisterously knocking over chairs
as they chased a ball of scrap paper,
which served as a football, around.

The new girl smiled shyly, every time someone looked
vaguely in her direction for a second.
She tried to look calm, collected, composed and confident
- but it was hard.
Imagining herself this time last year
back in Chester, a lively popular girl, the centre of attention.
Not an outsider.

But then something interrupted her thoughts.
A face smiling at her, chatting to her.
'What's your name? Do you want to talk to us?' it asked.
Or was she imaging it?
No she realised, she wasn't dreaming.
This person was interested in her - someone was talking to her.
The lump disappeared from the back of her throat
as the worries disappeared from her body.
'Yes,' she replied, 'I would.'
The new girl was beaming as she joined a huddle.

Jenny Mason (13)

THE ROCKING CHAIR OF TIME

The rocking chair of time
moves backwards, to and fro.
With mother nature sitting in it;
trying hard to sew.

Each stitch is like a person
weaving through their life.
Meeting other people
encountering some strife.

Without one, there is nothing.
Yet one is not enough.
Together they make a picture
which must take the rough and tough.

The rocking chair of time
moves backwards, to and fro
it stops for no one and nothing
and this we all must know.

And once we understand this
this will be a better place.
We'll need no one to watch us;
Mother Nature - rest in grace!

Jenni Abel-Dedman (13)

INSIDE MY HOUSE . . .

The wind howls like a lost dog
The trees shudder
The rain pours thick and fast onto the hard concrete outside.
And I am alone
Inside my house, wondering when it will end.
Wondering when I can get out.
I read a book trying to focus on something else.
But it only makes things worse.
I lie down staring at the ceiling, counting the squares.
And slowly . . . I start to fall asleep.

Sian Walker (13)

THOUGHTS

Thoughts of the breeze on a warm summer day,
Thoughts of the trees in the bright month of May.
Thoughts of a sweetheart far, far away,
These are the thoughts in my mind.

Thoughts of red noses from the cold of the snows,
Thoughts of the ice when the cold wind blows.
Thoughts of the warmth from the fire that glows,
These are the thoughts in my mind.

Thoughts of crisp brown leaves fresh fallen on the ground,
Thoughts of the dew on the grass all around.
Thoughts of robins chirping, my favourite sound.
These are the thoughts in my mind.

Reah Holmes (13)

CHRISTMAS DAWN

Before the stars disappeared
Before the winter morn.
Before the earliest cock-crow
Jesus Christ was born.

Priest and King lay fast asleep
In silent Jerusalem.
Young and old lay fast asleep
In the crowded Bethlehem.

Saint and angel, ox and ass
Keeping a watch together.
Before that Christmas dawn
In that winter long ago.

Let us kneel with Mary
With Joseph bent and hoary,
With saint and angel, ox and ass
To hail the King of Glory . . .

Hannah Goodwin (13)

THE CORAL REEF

Under the Caribbean Sea
is a truly wonderful sight.
Conch shells with music like bells
Playing away through the night.

Myriads of colours,
never seen on the shore.
Sparkling like diamonds
on the glistening sea floor.

Coral inhabits the water,
oscillating with the waves.
The octopus moves like an earthworm
as the tide goes into the caves.

Irregular shapes, irregular patterns,
complex beyond belief.
Unique like snowflakes
in the magnificent Coral Reef.

Catherine Wilson (13)

ALL INSECTS GREAT AND SMALL

To me a ladybird is a beetle with measles,
A wasp is a fly with a contagious disease.
A mosquito is an insect with a straw up its nose,
And greenflies are simply garden peas.

Worms are just fat strawberry laces
And dragonflies are toothpicks with wings.
As butterflies emerge from their cases
The dawn chorus just starts to sing.

Carly Telford (11)

THE BOY BY THE SEA

Gentle waves break softly, over smooth golden sand.
A young boy squats in the shallow water.
Tousled dark hair, flops lazily over one eye.
He has tanned skin, and his fingernails are stubby and ragged.
His face is kind. I wonder what he is thinking.
Sparkling brown eyes stare towards the rising sun,
Like a hungry predator watches its prey - silently.
As he looks out to sea, dolphins leap and bound
In the light from the golden sun
Dancing on the waves.
As far out as the child can see,
Where cornflower blue sky meets shimmering turquoise water,
A little fishing boat bobs up and down
On the calm surface of the water.
But who knows what strong, outward currents lie beneath the surface.
Strong, yet silent, and hidden from view.
Like a character behind a face you never studied carefully enough.
The boy shivers, the water round his ankles is much deeper now.
He wraps his coat around himself, stretches and stands up.
He trudges off the disappearing beach
Leaving a forlorn looking trail of footprints behind him.
Maybe he has a happy family, a warm fireplace and a cosy home
to go back to.

Maybe he doesn't.
How would I know
I'm only a seagull . . .

Abi Gleek (11)